Books Ablaze

and Other Historical Stories
You've Got to Hear!

BOOKS ABLAZE

and Other Historical Stories You've Got to Hear!

IRENE HOWAT

CF4•K

DEDICATION
For Stuart

10 9 8 7 6 5 4 3 2 1
© Copyright 2012 Christian Focus Publications
ISBN 978-1-84550-781-7

Published in 2012 by
Christian Focus Publications, Geanies House, Fearn, Tain,
Ross-shire, IV20 1TW, U.K.
Text by Irene Howat

Cover design by Daniel van Straaten
Cover illustration and inside illustrations
by Fred Apps
Printed and bound by Bell and Bain, Glasgow

Scripture quotations marked (esv) are from The Holy Bible,
English Standard Version, copyright © 2001 by Crossway
Bibles, a division of Good News Publishers. Used by
permission. All rights reserved.

CONTENTS

DREADFUL DIOCLETIAN

Are you ever given a hard time because you go to church or Sunday School? If you are being brought up in a Christian home, you may sometimes find that you are teased about this. But if you had been brought up in a Christian home in Nicomedia in the reign of Emperor Diocletian, you would have had a very hard time indeed. Here are five facts about Diocletian.

1. A.D. 245 – A little boy was born to a freed slave and his wife in the country that is now Yugoslavia. At that time the land was called Illyricum. The couple named their son Diocles.

2. As a young man Diocles joined the Roman Army. He rose through the ranks unusually quickly. Roman soldiers were not gentle people and they didn't get promotion for being kind and thoughtful. Diocles fought in the Persian War.

3. On 17th September in the year A.D. 284, when he was thirty-nine years old, Diocles (now called Diocletian) was appointed Emperor after being elected by the Roman Army.

4. He was a strong and a violent man, known to have killed with his own hands.

5. Diocletian worshipped the Roman gods, who were idols and not gods at all.

Imagine that you are a Christian in Nicomedia in the year A.D. 299. News reaches your town that Diocletian, who is in Antioch, has asked his fortune tellers what's going to happen in the future. They are unable to tell him and he decides that it is the Christians in the city who are stopping his fortune tellers from doing their work! So he orders all members of the Imperial Court and all soldiers in the Army to sacrifice to the Roman gods or leave their jobs. Of course, the Christians can't do that. They know that there's only one God, the Creator of all things and the Father of our Lord Jesus Christ. Many lose their jobs in the two or three years that follow. Some lose their lives.

While this is happening, it's as though Diocletian is giving all the good jobs to men who hate Christians. Imagine you are a member of the newly-built church in Nicomedia. You hear that the enemies of Jesus are being given important jobs in government. Bad things are happening to Christians and the people in the church know that worse things might follow. They hear that Diocletian is going for advice to an oracle of the Roman god Apollo (an oracle was a kind of priest who spoke for an idol god). The oracle says that the great god Apollo can't give advice because of 'the just on earth' and Diocletian decides that 'the just on earth' are Christians!

Had you lived in Nicomedia then, the 23rd of February A.D. 303 would have been a day to remember for very sad reasons.

That day Diocletian orders that the lovely new Christian church in the city should be completely destroyed. Not only that, he orders that all the books in the church should be taken out and burned.

Can you begin to imagine what it's like to see your church taken apart and destroyed? It must have been terrible. But how much worse it would have been to see God's Word, the Bible, torn apart, set alight and burned into flakes of grey ash.

The next day Diocletian issues another command. This time he says that throughout the entire Empire all Christian places of worship (some of them churches, many of them homes) are to be totally destroyed. Every single sheet or scroll of Christian writing is to be burned. Not only that, but Christians are told they cannot meet with one another for worship.

Emperors may pass all kinds of laws, but do you think if you had been there in February A.D. 303, you would have obeyed Diocletian? Or might you have met up with your Christian brothers and sisters in secret to pray for God's help? Of course that's what the Christians did in Nicomedia!

Diocletian probably saw fires burning and smiled as he thought of the holy books going up in flames. He was not nearly so happy when part of the Imperial Palace also caught fire! I imagine that the Christians in the city knew from the time they heard of the blaze that they'd be blamed for it, and they were, even though a legal investigation couldn't find out who started it. As February turned into March Christians in the city, and in the Empire, were treated very cruelly. Some faced death rather than sacrifice to Roman gods, and Diocletian thought up many unspeakable ways of killing them. But there was something that he didn't know. When each of these martyrs died, they went straight to be with Jesus in heaven.

Two weeks and two days after the first fire in the Imperial Palace in Nicomedia there was a second one. It was decided that the palace and the city were unsafe and not long afterwards Diocletian left.

Although he left, the Christians were still treated harshly. Roman soldiers ordered them to make sacrifices to idols. Ministers were especially picked out for persecution. Persecution is when Christians are treated badly, sometimes even killed, for believing in the Lord Jesus Christ.

Now imagine that the year is A.D. 311. How do you think the Christians react to the most recent news? After years of persecuting believers, the authorities decide that it hasn't been effective and that the persecution should stop. Then later on that year there is more news. Diocletian has died. There is even a possibility that he took his own life. How do you think the Christians feel about that? Do you think they rejoice to be rid of him? Or might it be that there is a deep sadness that he died not believing in Jesus?

13

BURN THEM!
EMPEROR'S ORDERS!

After Jesus died and rose again, the Christian church grew very quickly. Church leaders gathered together the Old Testament (which was the Bible Jesus used) and all the Christian papers for the early church. Among them were four life stories of Jesus, and letters to the new young churches. Eventually, after more than 200 years, it was decided which of the new papers should be included in the New Testament and that has never changed. Of course, until this was done some people came up with wrong ideas about Christianity. And even after the Bible was complete, men still produced some strange teachings. Imagine you are in Alexandria in Egypt about the year A.D. 320. Here is a conversation that might have taken place then.

'I'm really very concerned about some Bible teaching,' said one church leader. 'It doesn't seem to come from the Bible at all.'

'Are you talking about Arius?' his friend asked.

'Yes, I'm afraid I am. Have you heard what he's saying?'

'I've heard bits and pieces, but I've not paid much attention. Maybe you'd better tell me about it.'

The church leader sighed. He didn't want to be too critical, but he knew that Arius was wrong because what he was teaching was not in the Bible.

'Well, Arius says that Jesus has not always existed. He teaches that God created Jesus, and therefore God is greater than Jesus.'

'But that's not what the Bible says,' puzzled his friend. 'The Bible is quite clear that Jesus has always been, that he had no beginning and will have no end, that Jesus IS God.'

'Exactly! So what do we do about it?'

These are not the only two Christians concerned about what Arius is saying. The Roman Emperor then was Constantine the Great. He succeeded Diocletian. Now Constantine was very different from Diocletian, who had persecuted Christians. And the reason the new Emperor was different was that he became a Christian himself! Immediately he ordered that the persecution of Christians should stop, and what the Emperor said was law. Constantine also did all he could to spread the good news about Jesus. When he realised that Arius was causing problems, he called for a meeting to be held in Nicaea in A.D. 325. Imagine being involved in planning that meeting.

'How are we going to let all the church leaders know about it?' someone asks.

'We'll have to send letters by hand to them all. Now, where will they have to go?'

'Well, there's Egypt and Greece to start with.'

'And Israel.'

'Remember Syria and east of that.'

'Yes, and these are just the oldest churches. There are all the newer ones as well.'

'This is going to be a huge operation,' one man sighed.

The minister next to him smiled. 'If anyone has the means to do it, the Emperor certainly does.'

'That's good,' another said, 'for I understand that 1,800 orders to attend are going out!'

'What! How is the number so high?' someone asked.

'Well, the Emperor has told each leader that he can bring two ministers and three deacons.'

So dozens of men set out on horseback, mule and on foot with the command to attend. Messengers sailed across the Mediterranean Sea in all directions.

Eventually the great day came in May A.D. 325 and the huge gathering began. Constantine himself was 'there clothed in glittering raiment and adorned with gold and precious stones.' It was quite an occasion!

The main topic of discussion was what Arius was teaching about the Lord Jesus Christ not being as great as God the Father. It was debated for days on end. Eventually it was decided to write a clear statement about what the Christian church believed. The cleverest of all those who were at the Council worked on the project. Eventually, on 19th June the members, nearly 1,800 of them, gathered to hear the statement. And here it is. It is called the *Nicene Creed*.

We believe in one God the Father Almighty, Maker of heaven and earth, and of all things visible and invisible. And in one Lord Jesus Christ, the only-begotten Son of God, begotten of the Father before all worlds, God of God, Light of Light, Very God of Very God, begotten, not made, being of one substance with the Father by whom all things were made; who for us men, and for our salvation, came down from heaven, and was incarnate by the Holy Spirit of the Virgin Mary, and was made man, and was crucified also for us under Pontius Pilate.

He suffered and was buried, and the third day he rose again according to the Scriptures, and ascended into heaven, and sitteth on the right hand of the Father. And he shall come again with glory to judge both the quick and the dead, whose kingdom shall have no end.

Some time after the Council of Nicaea, Arius wrote a letter to Constantine that made him very angry. As a result, Constantine issued an order that all Arius's books had to be burned.

Why was it necessary for the Council of Nicaea to agree on what the Bible means? Well, if every footballer played to his own rules, the game would be total chaos. God's rule book is the Bible and the creed puts its teaching in a simple form to avoid misunderstanding in the church. If football rule books contained wrong rules they would have to be destroyed, so Arius's books with their wrong teaching about Jesus were best burned.

BOOKS ABLAZE!

Imagine it is England in the fourteenth century. The printing press hasn't been invented, and all books are written by hand. Of course, it takes ages to write a book so they are amazingly expensive. Only those who are very rich indeed can afford to own any. Now, imagine that you want to learn about the Lord Jesus. You can't afford a Bible and, in any case, you've never learned to read.

So you go to church and hear about Jesus. However, there's a problem. Many of the priests in English churches at this time are just like you – they can't read! What they know about the Bible, they've learned from other people and they are just passing it on to you in church each Sunday.

There's another problem. At this time the church throughout Europe is in a bad state. Most church leaders don't want people to read the Bible. It suits them fine that men and women can't read, or aren't able to afford Bibles for themselves. These dishonest men want to use the church for their own good rather than to tell others the news that Jesus is the one and only Saviour.

That's what life was like when John Wycliffe was born in 1324. John's home was in Yorkshire, in the north of England. When he was a young man he went to Oxford to study and it was while he was there that he met other young men like himself. If you had overheard them talking the conversation might have gone like this.

'The more I think about it, the more worried I am about what the church is teaching.'

'What do you mean?'

'Well, we're told that we can't pray directly to God; priests or saints have to pray for us. Now, in the New Testament I've read that I can pray to God through Jesus Christ, not through priests.'

'What worries me is that the Bible says that if we believe in the Lord Jesus Christ and confess him to others, then we'll be saved and go to heaven. The church says that we can maybe go to heaven if we believe the church's teaching. But we might end up spending eternity in purgatory.'

'And where does it teach about purgatory in the Bible? That's what I want to know.'

The young men sit and shake their heads. They all know that purgatory isn't in the Bible. The church teaches that there is a place called purgatory where people go when they die. Only those who are amazingly good go to heaven. To get out of purgatory the church teaches that friends and relations must pray prayers, or give the church money, to get them to heaven.

'The real problem,' says John Wycliffe, 'is that most people can't read the Bible for themselves. Even if they can read English, they still can't read the Bible for the only legal Bible is in Latin.'

'True enough,' his friend replies. 'What good is someone reading, *"sic enim dilexit Deus mundum ut Filium suum unigenitum daret ut omnis qui credit in eum non pereat sed habeat vitam aeternam"* when what they need to know is that, "God so loved the world that he gave his one and only

Son, that whoever believes in him shall not perish but have eternal life."'

'What we need is a Bible in English that can be easily read and totally understood.'

'Shoosh!' one of the more nervous young men says. 'That kind of talk is enough to have us thrown into Oxford prison!' And so it was.

John and his friends were serious men and clever too. It took them a long time, but they translated the whole of the Latin Bible into English. The Old Testament was originally written in Hebrew and the New Testament in Greek, but it had all been translated into Latin in the early fifth Century. This Latin version of the Bible was called the Vulgate.

At first, some church leaders in England supported the work John Wycliffe was doing. Apart from wanting the Bible in English, they weren't at all happy with the church in Rome because they had to send vast sums of money there every year.

But as the years passed they lost their enthusiasm even though ordinary men and women did not. It was a strange time to be living in England.

Because he was determined that people should have the Bible in their own language, John Wycliffe became very unpopular indeed with the church authorities. In fact, one archbishop wrote of him, 'that wretched and pestilent fellow, the son of a serpent ... filling up the measure of his malice

by devising the expedient of a new translation of the scripture into the mother tongue.' Eventually, in 1380, John was condemned as a heretic and he was expelled from Oxford two years later. In 1384 he died and went home to heaven.

Imagine you are living back in those days. Just because John Wycliffe has died you don't stop wanting to read the Bible in English, do you? Some followers of Wycliffe, they are known as the Lollards, continue the work he was doing and become just as unpopular as he had been.

Now, you are going to need to use a lot of imagination for the final (and the fiery) part of the story. You are in the archbishop's palace on the Hradschin in Prague (in what is now the Czech Republic) and it is 1410. A great number of priests have gathered in the courtyard and a fire is being prepared. You watch as the wood is laid out, smaller sticks first and then larger branches that will blaze well. A man moves forward with a burning torch and reaches out towards the kindling which catches light straight away. You can be sure that those who built the fire used the driest wood in order to give the best blaze. The little sticks crackle and spark and you watch as the flames leap and dance.

Then books and manuscripts are thrown into the fire. The priests seem to be enjoying themselves as each paper catches light and the blaze grows brighter still.

'How many are we burning?' you hear someone ask.

'More than 200 manuscripts,' is the reply.

'Did Wycliffe write them all?' the first man queries, surprised at the thought.

'No,' says his companion. 'But we're burning all the manuscripts we can find that have anything at all in them written by Wycliffe.'

Just imagine that blaze!

Back in England, that same year, Wycliffe's books were burned in the city of Oxford where he had lived and worked most of his life. Two years later his books were burned in a bonfire in front of the Basilica of St Peter's in Rome.

Of course, men could build great fires and burn books. They could even burn the Bible, but they could not stop people reading it, and read it they did. Things were changing and God was behind the change. The next 200 years were going to be hard for Christians, but a new and more Bible-based church would come out of it.

Even in the twenty-first century there are people groups that don't have the Bible in their own languages. Missionary organisations such as Wycliffe Bible Translators sometimes have to create scripts for languages that have never been written!

BURNT FINGERS

William Tyndale lived at a very exciting time as far as books were concerned, because the printing press was invented not very long before he was born. So before introducing you to William, there is someone else you have to meet. His name is Johann Gensfleisch, which translates from German to English as John Gooseflesh. Poor boy! It's not surprising that he later changed his name to Johann Gutenberg, and the name Gutenberg has a special place in history because of him.

The following story is told, and I cannot vouch for its truthfulness, but you can imagine it anyway. Picture yourself as young Johann out in your garden. As you have nothing better to do, you carve the letters of your name out of the bark of a tree. Then you gather up all the letters of the words Johann Gensfleisch and take them inside. You settle down beside the fire to arrange the letters when one of them falls from your hand into a pot of purple dye that had been on the fire to boil. You pick it out carefully, for the dye is still very hot, and drop it again right away in order not to burn your fingers. The dye-covered letter drops on to a piece of vellum and you leave it there to cool. When you risk picking it up again you discover that it has made the shape of the letter on the vellum.

Now you might think that's just the story of a careless boy playing too near a fire. But as he grew up Johann remembered what happened that day and thought about it.

He was a man before it sparked off an amazing idea in his head. And the idea was this. If he could cut out tiny letter shapes in wood, he could then dip them in ink and press them on to paper to print them. And if he could make a frame just the right size to hold rows of tiny letter shapes, he could put the letters in the right order in the frame to spell words, fasten them in very tightly indeed and then press the frame into ink before placing it on paper to print what he had written.

Of course, he had to remember to carve the wooden letters backwards and to put them into the frame backwards too or the print would turn out the wrong way round. If he carved the letters of his name the right way round and put them in the frame the right way round, it would be backwards when it was printed. This took quite a bit of working out!

Johann worked away at his idea and eventually built the first printing press that used moveable wooden type. And the very first book that was printed on it was the Bible in Latin. It became

known as the Gutenberg Bible and it was printed around 1452, the exact date is not certain. One hundred and eighty copies of the Gutenberg Bible were printed, 135 on paper and forty-five on vellum. The Bible had 1,272 pages and the paper on which it was printed was handmade. The average page had 2,500 letters printed on it, that's 2,500 individual letter shapes, carefully arranged back to front in a frame before being inked and pressed on to the paper.

Over forty years later, in England, William Tyndale was born. As a young man he studied the New Testament in Greek, the original language in which it was written. And he realised that the Vulgate (the Latin version of the Bible that had been printed by Johann Gutenberg), was not as good a translation as it might be. William decided to translate the Greek New Testament into English so that even a plough boy could understand it. But William had a problem. He had plenty of brains and a great deal of knowledge, but no money. And he couldn't begin his great project without someone to pay for it. Deciding to find help in London, he set out for the capital city hoping to see Bishop Tunstal, the Bishop of London. This man was well known for being generous to educational things. Sadly, Bishop Tunstal wanted nothing to do with the idea. Not only that, William discovered that he wouldn't be allowed to do the translation work in England! However, one man he met in London, a cloth merchant, encouraged William to follow his vision and gave him some money to help get him started.

In 1524, when he was not quite thirty years old, William Tyndale left on a ship for Hamburg, and from there he went to Cologne where he worked long hours on the translation. Imagine you are there. William has very little money and the work is long and wearisome, especially because he works in a cold room with poor lighting. He wraps himself up as well as he can and works for hours and hours, translating from Greek to English.

William reads the Greek carefully.

He translates each word and works out its meaning before deciding that the best translation is, *'As Iesus walked by the see of Galile he sawe two brethren: Simon which was called Peter and Andrew his brother castynge a neet into the see for they were fisshers and he sayde vnto them folowe me and I will make you fisshers of men. And they strayght waye lefte their nettes and folowed hym.'* Isn't it interesting to see English as it was written then?

Imagine how thankful and excited William must have been when the translation work was done and the printer in Cologne was ready to print! And then imagine how upset he was to discover that a man named Cochloeus – an enemy of the work he was doing – knew all about it. Cochloeus had bribed one of the printers! William Tyndale gathered together all of the work, headed out of Cologne and went to the city of Worms where the printing was eventually done. What a relief!

But how was he to get the English New Testaments to England? You'll remember that he had met a cloth merchant in London who gave him some money. Now that man and his friends had ideas and opportunities.

'Wrap some New Testaments in bales of wool and send them over in my ship,' one merchant wrote. 'Put some in my sacks of grain,' wrote another. That's exactly what William did.

Picture the scene at London docks. Merchants from different trades in London are there to meet the ships carrying supplies. Men haul sacks of grain off the ships. Others trundle great bales of wool on carts along the quayside. The merchants are smiling, pleased that their goods have arrived safely. But some smile because they know that inside their carefully wrapped goods are even more carefully wrapped English New Testaments and they can hardly wait to read them!

Of course Tunstal eventually heard that William's New Testaments had reached England and he was not pleased. He preached a sermon against it at St Paul's Cross in London, saying that Tyndale 'had translated the New Testament naughtily'! Of course, the more the bishop ranted and raved about the English translation, the more people wanted to read it! Silly man!

Imagine Bishop Tunstal coming up with what he thinks is a great idea. 'I'll buy all the books myself and burn the lot!' he decides.

So he searches among the merchants until he finds one who will agree to help.

'It will cost you a lot of money,' Merchant Packington tells him.

'I don't care,' Tunstal replies. 'It will be money well spent.'

What he doesn't know is that Merchant Packington is a friend of William Tyndale. And when William hears of the plan, he agrees to it. He sells New Testaments to his friend who sells them on to Bishop Tunstal. He is so pleased with himself over the next few days as he arranges to have a huge bonfire at St Paul's Cross in London. Tunstall's plan is to publicly burn all Tyndale's books. What a sad person Bishop Tunstal was, to think that he could destroy God's Word!

You see, William Tyndale knows something that Bishop Tunstal doesn't. There are some mistakes in the first printing of the English New Testament. The money Tunstal gives to burn these copies will pay for the mistakes to be corrected and another, bigger, printing done!

A further mistake that the bishop makes is that he burns the books in public in the centre of the great city of London. Everyone's talking about it, and what he does just advertises Tyndale's work. More people than ever now want to read the New Testament in English that is so simple that a plough boy can understand.

THE FIRE THAT DIDN'T HAPPEN

You may have been at a 5th November bonfire and enjoyed the sights and sounds of fireworks. It's a curious thing, but bonfire night reminds us of a fire that didn't happen! But I wonder if you know that by having a 5th November bonfire you are obeying a law passed in 1607. That's when the British government passed the Observance of 5th November Act.

To discover more we have to go back to the Duck and Drake Inn in The Strand in London. It's Sunday 20th May, 1604. Picture the scene. Five men sit round a table, they talk quietly in order not to be overheard. You strain your ears and catch just a few phrases.

'... want a Catholic on the throne ... Protestant like James I who ...'

'... to the continent ... plan to ...

'I can arrange ... gun powd ... enough ... for that ... Parliament ...'

King James I, the Scottish king,[1] who had recently become King of England as well, was a Protestant and did not like the Roman Catholic Church and its power in the country. He even ordered all priests to leave England! Of course, that made English Catholics very insecure and

---

[1] Although he was James I of England, he was actually James VI of Scotland!

unhappy. No doubt many Roman Catholics met to discuss the problem. But the men in the Duck and Drake were different; they were approaching their problem in such a spectacular way that it would be remembered over 400 years later. Had you heard all of their conversation it might have gone something like this.

'We want a Catholic on the throne, not a Protestant. We especially don't want a Protestant like King James who seems to hate everything Catholic,' whispers one man to his friend.

'I couldn't believe my ears when I heard he's banishing all our priests to the Continent,' one of the others shakes his head solemnly.

'I don't know if you'd be interested,' whispers the man on his right, 'but I'm toying with a plan to blow up King James. We would then have a Catholic queen and our priests would all be back on the next ship across the English Channel.'

'How would you do that?' someone asks.

The conspirator smiles. 'With enough gunpowder we could blow up the Parliament building. And if we did it on a day that King James was there ... well, he might even be killed.'

'Could you really get enough gunpowder for that?' one of the men asks, beginning to take the idea seriously.

'Yes, my friend,' the conspirator declares. 'I can get enough gunpowder to blow Parliament to bits, taking King James in bits with it!'

One of those men was Guy Fawkes, an expert with explosives.

The following month the conspirators gained the use of a house very close to where Parliament met. Were they planning to dig a tunnel from one building to the other? There has been much talk about that over the years, but no tunnel has ever and Other Historical Stories You've Got To Hear

been found. Instead they managed to get the use of a cellar right under where Parliament met!

If you had been in London on 20th July, 1605, in that dark cellar you would have found twenty barrels of gunpowder stashed there. By the next day another sixteen would have been smuggled in. A total of thirty-six barrels of gunpowder was a huge explosion waiting to happen. Listen to the conversation you might have overheard.

'Do you feel safe here?' one plotter asks another.

His companion laughs. 'I'll only feel safe when Parliament and the King go up in smoke – with me safely on the other side of the River Thames!'

'I was thinking. Our plan is to blow up the building at the grand opening of Parliament. It really will be a grand opening for it'll have no roof on it when we've done our job. It will be open to rain, hail and snow!'

49

'It's a bit early in the year for snow,' his companion tells him. 'And I'm glad that this will all be over long before winter comes. We seem to have been plotting and planning for ages.'

But due to a change in

circumstances the plot had to wait until there might very well have been snow on the ground. There was a threat of plague in London that summer. Two years earlier in 1603 the plague had been so bad that 30,000 Londoners died. When, in 1605, it was thought that the plague was about to strike again, the opening of Parliament was postponed till November!

That wasn't the only problem. In August, when Guy Fawkes and another man named Thomas Wintour went to check on the gunpowder, they discovered that it had decayed! More had to be brought and the new barrels were covered with firewood to hide them. Two months later, in October, the final details were decided.

'Right, let's go over exactly what's going to happen,' one of the conspirators says.

'Parliament is opening on 5th November and the King will be there. That's our big chance and our big day,' whispers another of the men.

Guy Fawkes says his piece. 'I light the fuse, a long one, and escape over the Thames to watch the fireworks from the other side.'

'Meanwhile, up north, Princess Elizabeth will be captured in order to be crowned Queen!'

On 29th October, Lord Monteagle, a Member of the House of Lords, received a letter. Part of it read: *'Retyre youre self into yowre contee whence yow maye expect the event in safti for ... they shall receyve a terrible blowe this parleament.'*

Lord Monteagle was being warned to escape for his life! When he showed the letter to King James, the King ordered the cellars under Parliament to be searched. The search was made just after midnight on 5th November ... when Guy Fawkes was caught leaving! Imagine you are there and see his arrest.

'What's your name?' the man who captured Guy Fawkes demands.

'John Johnson,' lies Fawkes.

'What are you doing with these explosives?'

'It was to blow you Scotch beggars back to your native mountains!' sneers Guy Fawkes.

It didn't take long to imprison Fawkes in the Tower of London. That night the Lieutenant of the Tower reported that John Johnson 'told us that since he undertook this action he did every day pray to God he might perform that which might be for the advancement of the Catholic Faith and saving his own soul.'

Had you been in London on 5th November 1605 you would have seen, not Parliament in flames, but bonfires lit all over the city to celebrate the safety of the King. Guy Fawkes and those of his fellow conspirators who were caught were tried and executed. It was shortly after that, that Parliament passed The Observance of 5th November Act which remained in force until 1859.

SETTING THE HEATHER ON FIRE

Imagine yourself in Scotland in 1638. It's Sunday 28th February and you are at a service in Greyfriars Kirk in Edinburgh. It's meant to be rather a special service and you hear quite a bit of talk about it, even on your way to church. A conversation might have gone a little like this, though it would have been in Scots rather than English.

'I think it's terrible that the King is trying to make Scots worship using the English Prayer Book,' a man says sadly. 'We're Presbyterians and he's determined to make the Church of Scotland Episcopalian, like the English church.'

'What does Episcopalian mean?' a boy asks.

'It means run by bishops,' his father explains. 'And there are many Scots who think that might be all right south of the border, but it's certainly not all right for us.'

'What do you think?' asks the boy.

His father stops for a minute.

'Put it like this, the Church of Scotland is ruled by elders because that's what we believe the Bible teaches. And we don't want that changed.'

'But there's more to it than that,' the man's friend says. 'The King's ordering our ministers to read written prayers rather than to speak to the Lord themselves.'

The boy is puzzled about long words like Presbyterian and Episcopalian, but he certainly understands that Christian ministers are able to pray using their own words rather than reading prayers the King has approved!

Now imagine yourself going into church. The building is very, very full and a great crowd of people has gathered outside. Inside, many people are standing, some are sitting on benches and others on stools. The minister gets to his feet and starts to read from the new Prayer Book. There's a lot of muttering and scuffling around you and you are aware that the people are not happy, not very happy at all. Suddenly you see and hear an extraordinary thing.

'Wha daur say mass in ma lug!' shouts a woman, as she stands up, picks up her stool and throws it at the minister!

You look around and see that most of the people in the church seem to agree with her!

The woman's name is Jenny Geddes. She and they don't like the new Prayer Book one little bit. Crowds press into Greyfriars Kirk, all wanting to sign a document protesting to the King. Tens of thousands of people sign it, and many more sign other copies in different parts of Scotland. While some rich and powerful Scots are willing to obey the King, he's making big trouble for himself with Scottish Christians.

In 1643 there was civil war in England and King Charles I was removed from the throne. Oliver Cromwell became Lord Protector and he ruled the country. Things changed dramatically after that. Cromwell supported the Scottish Christians and it looked as if they would have freedom to worship God as they chose. But just fifteen years later, Cromwell died, Charles II came to the throne and the whole sad situation started up all over again.

Had you been alive then, these are the kind of fears you would have heard discussed.

'I can't believe that we're back to where we were fifteen years ago,' says old Tom.

'But it's worse now,' his friend, Wattie, says. 'The King has sent his own bishops up from England and his ministers too. All our ministers that want to preach about Jesus are being put out of their churches.'

Old Tom shakes his head. 'I never thought I'd live to see this day.'

Wattie agrees. 'Well they're welcome to come to my house and hold services there. If we can't hear the Gospel in churches, we'll hear it in houses and barns and out on the hills too, if needs be.'

And that's exactly what was needed before long. At first the new bishops allowed Scottish Covenanters (that is what they were called) to meet in other buildings, but that was then outlawed and they had to gather outside. Then it grew worse still and they weren't allowed to meet at all, at least, not legally. On 13th August, 1670 a law was passed that said that those who met in conventicles (meetings of Covenanters) out on the Scottish hills could be executed!

Imagine yourself at a conventicle nine years later at Skeoch Hill not far from Kirkudbright in south west Scotland. You are one of about 6,000 Christians gathered there for The Lord's Supper or

Communion. You meet round four rows of large boulders and these are used for the people as they come forward to take the bread and wine. Three Covenanters preach that day and the service goes on for hours. Only about 300 people can take Communion at one time, so you see queues of men and women, and young folk too, waiting to come forward to where the boulders are, to take their place at the Lord's Table.

The conventicle at Skeoch Hill was a peaceful one, but many were not. Imagine yourself at another one three years later. The preacher has just come back from Ireland, where he had had to escape for his life from the King's dragoons. His name is Alexander Peden. You are now in the remote hills of South Ayrshire. Try to imagine that you are one of the lookouts. The conventicle is meeting in a hollow in the hills and you, and several others, are lying flat to the ground on the ridges surrounding the hollow. You have been posted where you can see anyone coming, but where nobody coming can see you. You lie there watching for the least movement and listening to the psalms being sung behind you but not daring to look round even for a minute as the Covenanters are relying on you for their lives.

As your eyes check the skyline from left to right and from right to left, you listen to Alexander Peden preaching and your heart warms to hear how he talks about Jesus. Your pulse races later in his sermon when he tells the Covenanters that they might have to die for Jesus, they might see their homes burnt to the ground and their crops set on fire for the privilege of hearing the Bible preached.

You are getting so excited at Alexander Peden's sermon that you almost turn round, but don't. That's when you see a movement between two hills some distance from the conventicle.

You creep swiftly down below the rise and then race, bent almost double, to the next lookout, who comes to see what you have seen. It's the King's dragoons! The pair of you career down the hill towards the conventicle, shouting out your warning as you run. Alexander Peden doesn't finish preaching right away. Instead, he reminds the people of what he's just said. Some of you might be called on to die for your faith, some might be taken to prison, some might have their homes burnt and some have their crops set on fire. Then he prays for you and asks God to bless and be with each one of you as you part.

Then an extraordinary thing happens. It is as though the conventicle melts! People move away in their twenties and thirties until there is nobody there at all. But they don't all move quickly enough for there are dragoons coming from different directions having been told by an informer where you're meeting. You hear shots as some of those brave Christians are killed. And as you escape by going many miles round under the cover of bushes and along the hollows of springs, you see utter devastation. Cottages are ablaze, their thatched roofs having been torched by the dragoons. Corn and barley, almost ripe for harvest, is on fire with flames licking their way along the narrow rigs. And from time to time as you creep along under cover, you see men being led away by the dragoons and women and children standing wondering where their men are being taken and if they'll ever see them again.

Fires blazed all over the country areas of west and central Scotland and to a lesser extent in other parts of the country too. By 1686 Alexander Peden's home was a cave at the side of the River Lugar in Ayrshire. It was the only place he felt safe from the King's men. A day or two before he died, he was just able to get to his brother's house nearby. And even as that brave Covenanting leader died there, the dragoons were searching the farm's outbuildings.

And the end of the story? From 1680 to 1685 Christians were so seriously persecuted in Scotland that those years were called the Killing Times. But eventually the killings ceased and the fires stopped raging as Scottish Christians were once again allowed to worship freely and to hear the gospel preached by godly men in churches and without the use of the Prayer Book.

GONE, FOREVER

It's France. It's 1680. Your name is Pierre and your sister, who is four years older than you, is called Suzanne. Your father has a small farm and you are both helping with the bean harvest. Your dad told you to work together and not to stray from each other. His voice was so serious that you do exactly what you're told. After working all morning you sit down beside a wall for lunch. The wall shades you from the hot midday sun – and hides you from danger. Mum's bread and cheese are just what you need after a hard morning on the bean rows.

'Is it safe to talk here?' you ask your sister.

Suzanne looks puzzled. 'What do you mean?'

'Well, Dad says we have to watch what we say and where we say it. And if I try to ask him about the troubles, he shushes me as though walls have ears. I really do want to know what's happening. Will you tell me?' you plead.

Suzanne smiles in her annoying big-sisterly way.

'I think this wall's all right. No ears that I can see,' she says eventually. 'And I've told Dad that I think you're old enough to understand things. He's just trying to protect you.'

'But I'm nine,' you complain. 'I don't need protected.'

'Right,' Suzanne says, 'I will tell you. And when we get home I'll tell Dad you know.'

'You might get into big trouble,' you worry.

Your sister shrugs. 'That's my problem.'

You munch your way through your bread and cheese and listen carefully.

'You know that we are Protestants and that most people in France go to the Roman Church. Well, the Protestant church only started before the middle of last century. And it started because things had gone badly wrong in the church before that and some terrible things were happening.'

'What sort of things?' you ask.

Suzanne thinks for a minute. 'Let's just say that priests weren't preaching the Bible and they didn't actually want people to read it for themselves either. That made the church powerful and it wanted to stay that way.'

You aren't sure that you understand, but you don't interrupt.

'A great preacher who came from Noyon ...' says Suzanne.

'Noyon's not far from here!' you interrupt excitedly.

'That's right. Well, he came from Noyon and he discovered the wrong things that the church was teaching. His name was John Calvin.'

'That doesn't sound like a Noyon name,' you argue.

Suzanne laughs. 'Clever you! It's not. He was Jean Cauvin, but he went to be a minister and teacher in Geneva and that seems to be how they pronounce it there.'

You sit back and relax. This is an interesting story.

'Over a hundred years ago those Christians who believed the Bible, many who had studied under Calvin, started a Protestant church here in France. But the Roman Church didn't like that and there was much fighting between the two groups. Then, in 1572, an awful thing happened.'

'I don't remember it?' you say.

Suzanne smiles. 'Of course you don't. You weren't born! But I've heard about it and it was shocking. There was a Protestant royal wedding and many of our people went to Paris to celebrate. But Paris was mainly a Catholic city. At the Feast of St Bartholomew there was a terrible massacre and thousands of Huguenots were killed. It came to be called the St Bartholomew's Day massacre. Dad's great, great granddad was killed in Paris that day. I think that's why he can't talk about it.'

'But that was a long time ago,' you say. 'It's different now.'

'Yes and no,' is all Suzanne comments.

She eats her bread and cheese before going on with the story.

'We haven't had much trouble here for a long time,' your sister explains, 'but other parts of France have. And I'm afraid that it might come here again, but not yet.'

'Why not yet?' you ask.

'Because there's a law that says we have freedom to worship as we choose, but there's talk of that law being changed. Things could be very different then.'

'Is that what worries Dad and Mum?' you ask.

'Yes, I think it is. Do you want to ask any other questions?'

You have one that's been puzzling you for some time.

'I know we're Protestants,' you say, 'but we are also Huguenots. What's the difference?'

Suzanne smiles. 'That's not too hard to answer. It really boils down to Huguenots being French Protestants.'

'Well, I'm French,' you laugh, 'so I'm going to call myself a Huguenot.'

Five years later, in 1685, you hear shocking news. The law has been changed. Huguenots are no longer free to gather and worship. Not only that, there's news of brigades attacking Huguenot homes, evicting the people who live in them and then burning their houses to the ground as they watch. And the news gets worse, these burnings are coming nearer and nearer. It's not only houses that are burned, it's crops ready for harvest, and ... sometimes ... it's Christian people who refuse to go to the Roman church!

'Get up!' Dad's voice slices through your sleep.

'Get up and dressed NOW!'

You are on your feet before he's finished speaking.

'Where's Suzanne?' you ask.

'Suzanne's away, and we've got to move fast,' insists Dad, 'or we may not see her again!'

Your father has heard news that sends a chill down your spine. Several Huguenot homes round about have been torched and your church is blazing in the distance. You can see it through the night darkness.

'Get out and fill up the hay cart as high as you can. There are two children in the stable. Wrap them in sacks and hide them in the cart deep under the hay. Make sure they have space to breath and give them each a rag in case the dust makes them sneeze so that they don't make any noise.'

You don't need any more instructions. Plans have already been made and you know what you have to do.

You go over the fine details. 'I go as soon as day breaks. I take the donkey and cart, with the children hidden deep in the hay, as if I'm just doing my usual farm work and I take them to the Le Harivel house. From there someone else will take the cart to the next safe house.'

'That's right, my boy,' Dad says, 'and may God be with you all as you go.'

The worst thing for you is not knowing about Suzanne. But you understand why she had been rushed away as soon as news of the raids came. A terrible thing is happening to Huguenot girls her age if they are captured. They are often taken to convents and locked away, maybe for the rest of their lives! At the same time you feel proud that you are being trusted to get two Huguenot children to safety. The plan is that their parents will follow later in the day, but looking as if they were going to market. It would give the show away if they had their children going to market with them. Especially when the children should be at school.

You pack up the children and set off for the Le Harivels as soon as it is light. Along the way you meet a group of men you've never seen before. They question you. They pull some of the hay off the cart and one man pokes a stick right down through the hay. Your heart seems to stop beating but there is no sound from the children. Eventually the men let you go. You nearly faint with relief when you arrive and find your cargo all safe and well, if very, very frightened.

When night falls, you head back to your parents, desperate to hear news of Suzanne. But when you arrive there is a great fire raging where your house once stood. You can see other fires along the hillside where your Huguenot friends live. Dad and Mum are nowhere to be seen. Although you are just fourteen, you know exactly what you must do.

So, with nothing other than what you are wearing, you head north, walking by night and resting in safe places as soon as daylight comes. For the first few days you hide out in Huguenot homes where you are given food. Then you are

joined by others on the trek north, and they know the next lot of houses that you can shelter in. Night after night you travel and it takes over a week for your prayers to be answered, but they are. At one safe house you find your Dad, Mum and Suzanne! Your journey is a long one and it takes you out of France, never to return. Weeks later you arrive in Antwerp where Huguenots are welcome and free to worship according to the Bible. You have nothing except each other and your faith in Jesus as your Saviour. There are many others there like you, including some from your own village. It took a very long time, but now you can finally feel safe once again.

BIBLE VERSE

Blessed are you when others revile you and persecute you and utter all kinds of evil against you falsely on my account. Rejoice and be glad, for your reward is great in heaven, for so they persecuted the prophets who were before you.

Matthew 5:11-12 (ESV)

SHA KUEI-TZU!

Your imagination is going to take you to quite a different place now and to another century. Try to picture yourself in the 1880s in China. Imagine yourself listening to a conversation there between two men, one of them very angry.

'China used to be our country and it should be our country once again!'

'What do you mean?' his companion asks.

'I'll tell you what I mean,' the man says crossly. 'In the last hundred years people have come from different countries of the world and tried to take China over. You think about it! Who gets the riches that should be ours? It's the Japanese, the Dutch, the Spanish, the French, the British and the Russians. They've come in with their factories and their armies and taken the best areas of our country to develop for themselves.'

'I see what you mean,' agrees his companion.

The man was becoming angrier and angrier as he talked.

'There are millions of poor Chinese people while Chinese money is being bled out to make powerful people in other countries rich!'

'What do you think we should do about it?'

'What should we do about it? We should expel foreigners from our country and keep it for ourselves. And the first ones I'd expel would be Christians.'

'Why's that?' his friend asks. 'Surely they're the very ones who aren't taking wealth out of China to make themselves rich.'

'I'll tell you why!' the man is furious now. 'They're taking China out of China! They want to convert Chinese people to Christianity and that would change China forever. What they actually want to do is to make China a Christian country. How dare they! Why should we be a Christian country? We have our own religions and we don't want to change!'

The words were almost spat out!

The two men move away and you think about what you've heard. It's all a bit confusing. You know that Jesus said that his followers have to go

83

to every country and tell people about him. And you know that's good news because nobody can go to heaven unless they believe in the Lord Jesus. So you reckon there's a problem. If missionaries go to other countries to teach about Jesus, then they are taking good news, the best news in the whole world. And of course they hope that these other countries will become Christian. You'd never before thought of that being a problem, but it seems to be with some people.

China at that time was in a state of change. Many millions of peasant people held on to traditional beliefs. For example, they believed that the power of magic could protect them from foreign bullets and that martial arts could defend them from foreign armies, even the most powerful armies in the world. There was a group of people called the Boxers, and the angry man you heard was one of them. They wanted China to be what they thought it had always been and they wanted everyone else out, especially Christians. The Boxers saw Christians as a real threat to Chinese identity. And they were especially down on the 'secondary hairy ones,' which is what they called Chinese people who became Christians.

The Chinese name for the Boxers was The Society of Righteous and Harmonious Fists. They believed that by force they were doing what was right for China. Starting off as a secret society in Shandong in the north of China, the Boxers spread quickly, especially among those who believed that other countries were taking over their beloved land. The Society of Righteous and Harmonious Fists believed that they were possessed by spirits more powerful than other religions; some even thought they could train themselves to fly!

By the 1890s things had become very difficult indeed. The cry of 'Sha kuei-tzu!' was heard in Christian communities. It was the Boxer war cry

'Kill the devils!' and the devils they intended killing were first, Chinese Christians, and then missionaries who had come from other countries. In 1890 in the countryside south of Peking (that great city is now known as Beijing) Christian churches were burned to the ground, the homes of believers were torched, missionaries were

murdered and thousands of 'secondary hairy ones' were slaughtered because they believed in Jesus. Tragically, some 'secondary hairy ones' hadn't actually believed in Jesus at all, rather they followed the missionaries because of the help they were given by them.

By the time the 20th Century began, thousands of Christians had been killed and their homes burned to the ground. General Dong Fuxiang and the Muslim Kansu joined the Boxers. They went from house to house where they thought there were Christians. If they found any Chinese idols in the houses, they sat down and had tea, took anything they wanted, apologised and then left! But if they found no Chinese idols, they assumed the home was a Christian home and killed those who lived there before burning the place down. Needless to say, when they came across a church it was demolished or torched right away for they knew that there would be no Chinese idols inside it!

In the town of Honchau, there was a Chinese couple. The husband was known as Faithful Yen. When they were questioned by The Society of Righteous and Harmonious Fists they would not agree to worship Chinese idols rather than Jesus.

'Take them to the temple!' the order rang out, after they were interrogated.

Faithful Yen and his wife were dragged into the pagan temple and beaten. Then they were tied to a pillar and a fire was lit behind them. It was stoked with wood until their poor legs were terribly burned.

'More wood!' came the order, when the two brave Christians would not deny Jesus.

And their legs were burnt even more.

One of the Chinese soldiers who was on duty that day was so sickened by what was going on that he cursed the Boxers and paid for it with his life. Eventually on that terrible day Mrs Yen was set free, dreadfully injured as she was. Faithful Yen was dragged to the magistrate's house and then thrown into a dark prison cell with no medical treatment for his poor burnt legs.

The Boxer Rebellion, as it was called, was over by 1901, but it is estimated that it cost the lives of hundreds of missionaries and tens of thousands of Chinese Christians. Twentieth century China continued to be difficult for those who believed in the Lord Jesus Christ. And now we are in the twenty-first century. What's it like for believers in China today? It's still hard to be a Christian there. But whatever men and women do, they can't stop God working. Many people in China are becoming Christians, some say as many as 30,000 each day! In 2011 the world population was estimated to be 6,914,700,000 men, woman and children. Almost one in five of them (1,341,000,000) live in China and they need prayer that God will be with them.

KOMSOMOL
ANTI-CHRISTMAS

Imagine you are nine years old. You are in a twentieth-century Russian School. The lesson being taught there would not be like any you've ever had before.

'Boys and girls,' the teacher says, 'today we are going to talk about the stupidity of religion. You may hear someone talking about Jesus Christ as if he really existed. But he is only a character in a fairy tale book called the Bible. Does anyone here believe that Jesus Christ is real?'

The children sit silently. Some may come from Christian homes but they're not going to tell that to their teacher.

The teacher looks round the class, pleased that nobody is stupid enough to say that they think that Jesus is a real person.

'Who does believe in Jesus?' she asks.

Several hands go up.

'Very old people,' one boy suggests.

'Silly people,' says another.

'People who are ill in their minds,' adds a girl, knowing that was what she should say.

'That's right,' smiles the teacher. 'Stupid and crazy people believe the Bible. Imagine believing in a fairy tale!'

The children in the class laugh at the thought.

'Who else believes in Jesus?' she asks, determined to revise her lesson thoroughly.

'Those who hate our Motherland believe in Jesus,' another student tells her.

The teacher is pleased. He really has been listening to her lessons.

'That's right,' she praises him. 'But I'm surprised that you didn't all put your hands up. Now listen and I'll tell you once again.

'Americans and Britons are our enemies. They are both waiting to start a great war with our country. One day, we don't know when, soldiers will invade our beloved Motherland. They are stupid. They are so stupid that they believe in the fairy tale book the Bible, and they believe that Jesus is real. Do you hear what I say?'

The children all nod their heads and say yes.

In 1917, before these children were born, there was a revolution in Russia and after that it became a Communist country. Communists don't believe in God. In fact, until 1991, when Communism fell in Russia, children were taught terrible things about Christianity. The state even made films to spread lies about the faith. Churches were closed down. It was illegal to have or read the Bible. People could be put in prison, even killed, for teaching their children about the Lord. Teachers taught lessons just like the one in the story. Children even used words to do with Christianity as swear words.

Now, here's an odd thing. When the Communists were in power they still called the days of the week what they had always been called. And the word for Sunday in Russian is Voskresenie. For hundreds of years that has been the name used for Sunday in Russia. But it has a Christian meaning! The word Voskresenie means 'day of Resurrection' and it was called that because it was the day on which the Lord Jesus rose from the dead. So all through the years of Communism, every time Sunday was mentioned, the person who spoke referred to Jesus rising from the dead!

And here's another strange thing, Russian people celebrate Christmas on the 7th of January! So two weeks after your Christmas is over, Christmas is just beginning in Russia. Because it is a happy time the Communists knew that people would still want to celebrate even though they were being told that Jesus was just the hero of a fairy tale. What were they to do about it?

Imagine that you are in a Communist meeting in the 1920s. Strong and powerful men are discussing what to do about this problem. What might they be saying?

'We must work out how we can show people that religion is just for fools, that God doesn't exist,' says an army officer.

'I vote that we ban Christmas,' announces the man sitting next to him. 'If there's no Christ, there can't be Christmas.'

There's a great stamping of feet to show that the others agree with him. But one man doesn't agree.

'I think you'll have riots if you ban Christmas because everyone likes the holiday.'

'What do you suggest then?' someone asks.

The army officer has an idea. 'What about having an Anti-Christmas? We could call it a Komsomol Anti-Christmas.' (The Komsomol was the Communist organisation for young people).

The men discuss this idea and decide to go along with it. They make plans to hold Komsomol Anti-Christmases in hundreds of Russian cities.

Now you are in Moscow in January 1923, watching a long parade.

'Listen to the Komsomol choir!' the woman next to you says.

You listen and hear the tune of a Christmas carol, but the words are new.

Thy Komsomol Christmas

Restoring to the world the light of reason

Serving the workers revolution

Blooming under the five pointed star

We greet thee, sun of the Commune

We see thee on the heights of the future Russian

Komsomol, glory to thee!

The words are not about the birth of Jesus at all! They're about Communism!

You continue to watch what's happening.

Usually at Christmas there are floats with people dressed as shepherds and wise men and other characters from the Bible story. Today they are clowns making a fool of the

Bible and of the Lord Jesus Christ. Some of the horrible clowns carry Bibles and tear pages out of them! Men and women, and even boys and girls, carry bright-coloured banners that mock the Lord.

You follow the parade and discover that it stops at a huge bonfire. And you watch as life-sized dolls of Bible characters are thrown on the fire. Then the Bible pages are fed handful by handful into the flames. It's becoming a grotesque celebration of there being no God, almost a party. In fact, it is a party because even though the Communists don't believe in God, they still want to party at Christmas time.

Komsomol Anti-Christmas bonfires blazed in over 400 Russian cities in the 1920s but they didn't stop Christians celebrating the birth of the Lord Jesus Christ quietly in their own homes where they couldn't be seen or heard.

From 1917 until 1991 Communists tried to stamp out Christianity ... and failed. And when Communism fell in Russia in 1991, among the first people to travel into the country were Christians who wanted to take the good news about Jesus to the many millions of Russian people for whom the Bible had been the forbidden book for over seventy long years.

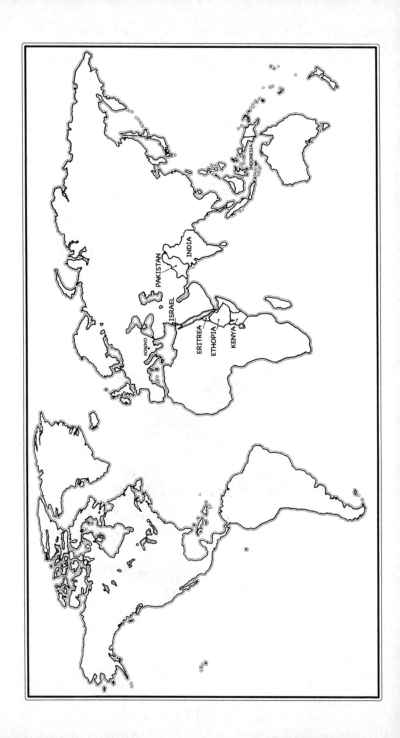

FIRES ARE STILL BURNING

That brings us right up to the twenty-first century, but the fires haven't stopped burning. For example, in 2008 Christian churches were burned down in several parts of the world.

Let's go first to the north east of India, to the state of Orissa. As most of the population (about 94%) are Hindu there are many beautiful temples there. Only a very small proportion of people are

Christians. The population of Orissa is about 40 million. Those going to church are mostly from the Oraon, Kharia and Munda people.

Sadly, there is a great deal of tension between some Hindu people and Christians. Swami Laxmananand Saraswati, head of the Vishwa Hindu Parishad (World Hindu Council), said in 2008, 'They want to convert people to Christianity and convert the country into a Christian land. We are opposed to that and that is the source of all disputes and fights.'

Because of the difficulties, Christians in Orissa tend to live near to each other. This gives protection in times of trouble. Imagine you are there in Orissa in September 2008 in a refugee camp set up by the State especially for Christians.

'Why are you here?' you might ask one of the young people in the camp.

'I had to run away from my village with my parents and brothers and sisters because we were in danger,' Pradeep explains.

'What kind of danger?' you ask.

Pradeep doesn't know where to begin his story.

'Christians here usually live in villages together. We do everything in our village: go to school, go to church, everything. From time to time it can be dangerous to leave the village because some Hindu people don't like Christians and we can be attacked.'

'Are all Hindu people like that?' is your next question.

Pradeep smiles. 'No, of course they're not. Most Hindu people don't mind us worshipping God. In fact, over the last few years many Hindu people have become Christians. My dad and mum were Hindu until they heard the good news about the

Lord Jesus Christ. Then they realised they were worshipping idols that couldn't help them and certainly couldn't take them to heaven when they die.'

'Wasn't it dangerous for them to become Christians?' you want to know.

'Yes,' Pradeep says. 'I've heard of some new Christians being forced to say that they've become Hindu again.'

'So how did you come to be here in a refugee camp?' you ask.

Pradeep explains that one day a group of angry thugs raided their village, and burned most of it to the ground. His family were members of a Baptist church and the church building was also trashed and burned.

Pradeep takes you to one of the village elders who is a leader in his church. You ask him to tell you about what has been happening recently.

'Where to begin ...?' the old man says. 'Where to begin?'

You wait until he gathers his thoughts together.

'I think it will be best if I just tell you the facts that I've heard,' the man decides. 'In August in Kandhamal over fifty Christians were killed and homes and churches were torched. Some of the people in this camp come from there and they told me about it. Then we heard news from the village of Balligada where twenty-five homes belonging to Christians were set on fire and others were burned in Phiringia and Sujeli. We are Baptists and we hear news of other Baptist churches being torched.'

'Do all the people come to refugee camps when their homes are burned down?' you ask.

The old man looks at you sadly.

'No,' he says. 'At the end of last year thousands of Christians ran away to the jungle for safety. But I don't think they are safe even there.'

Having heard Pradeep's story, and a little about the problems Christians face in some parts of the world, you decide to do some research of your own. Using the Internet, you look for all the news you can find about Christian persecution in 2008. You are shocked at what you discover.

January: Kenya – A mob attacked a church in Kiambaa and set it alight, killing around fifty people who were inside.

March: Ethiopia – Two churches were destroyed and burned.

March: India – In Orissa two houses belonging to Christians were set on fire and destroyed in Raikia, fifty in Balligada, three in Kakadabadi, thirty-five in Tikabali (Beheragano) and five in Chakapad.

April: Kosovo – A church was burned to the ground.

May: Israel – Christian books were set on fire by an extremist group in the city of Ohr Yehuda.

May: Indonesia – Three churches, 120 Christian homes and a school were burned to the ground.

June: Ethiopia – Some of the men who destroyed the churches in March were sentenced to life imprisonment.

August: India – Christians in Pirigada village were attacked and their houses burned. They escaped to the hills. When they returned they found a mob of at least 400 people demanding that they convert to Hinduism or be killed.

October: Eritrea – The Authorities confiscated and burned 1,500 Bibles belonging to high school pupils in Asmara. Eight of the students protested and were arrested.

December: Pakistan – Christians were white-washing their church in village Chak 77-RB, Lohekay, about thirty kilometres from Faisalabad. They went for a break leaving the church open. When they came back the Bible and Christian books had been burned. A note was left telling them to convert to Islam.

Pakistan – A twenty-year-old Christian woman was wrongly accused of tearing pages out of the Qur'an. She and her father were arrested. A mob pelted their home with stones before setting it alight.

December: Indonesia – About 500 people in Masohi, in the Moluccan Islands, clashed with police and local Christians. Forty-five homes, a church and a hall were set alight in the disturbance.

Christians who are persecuted are not alone because Jesus promises to be with all his people

all of the time. He says, 'And surely I will be with you always, to the very end of the age.' If you are a Christian, that promise is for you too. Perhaps sometimes people laugh at you for trusting in Jesus, or poke fun at you for going to church. If they do, remember that they laughed at Jesus and poked fun at him too. And Jesus remembers and he understands.

If you are not a Christian, this is a really good time to think about what Jesus has done for you. The Bible says, 'For God so loved the world that he gave his one and only Son, that whoever believes in him shall not perish but have eternal life.' God's one and only Son is Jesus and, if you ask him to forgive you and be your Saviour, that's what he'll do because he keeps all of his promises. Then, like Christians from all ages and from every country in the world, you can enjoy Jesus' company every day of your life – whatever happens to you - and look forward to seeing him face to face when you go to heaven.

BIBLE VERSE

You have heard that it was said, 'You shall love your neighbor and hate your enemy.' But I say to you, Love your enemies and pray for those who persecute you, so that you may be sons of your Father who is in heaven. For he makes his sun rise on the evil and on the good, and sends rain on the just and on the unjust.

Matthew 5: 43–45 (ESV)

CHRISTIAN FOCUS PUBLICATIONS

Christian Focus · Christian Heritage · CF4K · Mentor

Christian Focus Publications publishes books for adults and children under its four main imprints: Christian Focus, CF4K, Mentor and Christian Heritage. Our books reflect that God's word is reliable and Jesus is the way to know him, and live for ever with him.

Our children's publication list includes a Sunday school curriculum that covers pre-school to early teens; puzzle and activity books. We also publish personal and family devotional titles, biographies and inspirational stories that children will love.

If you are looking for quality Bible teaching for children then we have an excellent range of Bible story and age specific theological books.

From pre-school to teenage fiction, we have it covered!

Find us at our web page:
www.christianfocus.com

CF4·K
*Because you're never
too young to know Jesus*